DEVELOPING RESILIENCE IN YOUNG PEOPLE WITH AUTISM
USING SOCIAL STORIES™

DR SIOBHAN TIMMINS

T0299607

Jessica Kingsley *Publishers*
London and Philadelphia

First published in 2017
by Jessica Kingsley Publishers
73 Collier Street
London N1 9BE, UK
and
400 Market Street, Suite 400
Philadelphia, PA 19106, USA

www.jkp.com

Library of Congress Cataloging in Publication Data
A CIP catalog record for this book is available from the Library of Congress

British Library Cataloguing in Publication Data
A CIP catalogue record for this book is available from the British Library

ISBN 978 1 78592 329 6
eISBN 978 1 78450 643 8

Printed and bound by CPI Group (UK) Ltd, Croydon, CR0 4YY

This book is dedicated to my son Mark,
who faces all challenges with
an honesty, courage and dignity
that humbles me daily.

He is my inspiration.

Acknowledgements

I would like to thank Mark for giving his permission to publish his Social Stories™ so that other young people might benefit from them.

Special thanks must go to Carol Gray for devising and developing the invaluable Social Stories approach which has changed all our lives for the better and still continues to do so. My family and I will always be grateful for this amazing strategy.

Thanks too to the people who have helped Mark to overcome recent challenges, building his resilience: Lyndon Taylor, his coach at Colchester and District Fencing Club, and Joe Nutkins at Dog Training for Essex and Suffolk, who has trained Mark and Rosie together for five years to become an awesome agility and trick dog team!

Many thanks also to Jessica Kingsley for all her sound advice, and to Hannah Snetsinger, Emma Holak, Rob Rorison and all the team at Jessica Kingsley Publishers for all their patience and expert help.

Most of all I must thank my husband and family for their unfailing love and support.

Contents

Understanding the Perspective of Young People on the Autism Spectrum

In order to encourage the development of resilience in young people on the autism spectrum we first of all need to understand and respect their perspective of the world.

How we understand the world around us is governed by how our brain processes the vast amount of information streaming in through our senses. People on the autism spectrum process this information in a different way to people who are not on the spectrum (neurotypical people). As a result, they have a different perspective of life to neurotypical people and their responses to situations may therefore seem unexpected, unusual and sometimes even challenging to neurotypicals. Parents and professionals frequently note that the strategies that usually help neurotypical young people frequently fail for those who are on the autism spectrum. This may lead to the young person mistakenly being labelled as non-compliant or defiant. It is important to realise that this perspective of the world is as valid to the young person as our perspective is to us; it is not a choice he has made – he cannot choose to perceive in a different way. In our predominantly neurotypical world, life can be very tough for those with an autistic perspective.

Frequent negative social interactions and negative social experiences can lead to low self-esteem, increased anxiety and social isolation, with an impact on mental health.

There are three main validated theories that explain how neurotypical people process the clues surrounding them in order to have social understanding. Knowing how social understanding comes about helps us understand how different the perspective may be if these processes are not working as quickly or efficiently. The theories are called central coherence (Frith, 2003), theory of mind (Baron-Cohen, 1995) and executive function (Pennington and Ozonoff 1996; Goldberg *et al.*, 2005). More recently a fourth theory has been proposed by Dr. Peter Vermeulen called context blindness (Vermeulen, 2012). This theory unifies the other theories and in addition gives an explanation of the other features of autism not completely addressed by them, namely sensory and literal language difficulties.

The theories in more detail

Central coherence/context blindness

Neurotypicals are context sensitive and have strong central coherence. This means we are able to put together the socially relevant clues in a situation in order to make social sense of it. We continually pick up information from our surroundings and from others through our senses, and our brains instantaneously process this information, identifying the 'gist' or context of a situation. The context then focuses us only on the details that are socially relevant to that context, in preference to any other details present, in order to make social sense of a new or changing situation. All that is not socially relevant is faded into the background. Information is then matched and drawn from previous similar experiences stored in our memory. This instantly helps us with the current situation, identifying whether it is safe or dangerous, and importantly allowing us to predict what may happen next. This enables us to choose safe and effective responses to suit the situation. We do not even need to think about it – this all happens subconsciously, innately and intuitively.

In contrast, young people on the autism spectrum, despite being able to notice tiny details and changes around them, do not always accurately recognise and use the context. They therefore focus on details that are socially irrelevant, but which are instead particularly interesting for them. They are missing crucial social information. This results in a lack of awareness of the sort of social situation they are currently in, and consequently they are less likely to choose a safe and effective response. Instead a response is chosen that is related to the details they have focused on, and this may seem out of place and unexpected to those neurotypicals around them. Young people on the autism spectrum require time to consciously work out the context, time that is not available in the quick to and fro of a rapidly changing social interaction or situation. They can be described as having context blindness and weak central coherence. Similarly, they often have difficulty making social sense of the clues involved in facial expressions, tone of voice and body language in other people. They may be less able to discern how these clues give an idea of the emotion that person may be currently experiencing.

As a consequence of this difficulty with context and making sense of a social situation or interaction, our young people may be less able or unable to recognise when a situation is coming to an end and a new situation is beginning. Change becomes frightening and disturbing and results in huge anxiety. In order to relieve this anxiety our children may strive to control the people and objects in the environment and keep everything the same. They may feel reassured by structure and ritual, being soothed by repetitive activities like watching the same video clip over and over – perhaps the only time they can truly predict what is coming next.

Theory of mind

In addition to immediately grasping the context of a situation, neurotypicals are also able to be continually aware of what another person may be thinking, feeling, knowing or believing. This is often referred to as having theory of mind, and an absence or difficulty in this area is a common feature to all those on the autism spectrum. Having this ability allows us to be aware that we may be upsetting, annoying or boring another person and stimulates us to stop what we are doing, change topic or move away. This keeps us safe and effective in our interactions with other people. Without this ability, a young person will simply not have other people's thoughts and feelings in mind during his interactions with others. He may continue with a conversation for example, without taking turns to listen, oblivious to the other person's upset or boredom, or he may state a fact about another person's appearance or performance that is hurtful. This makes it difficult for him to make and keep friendships. Lacking mindfulness of what other people might know may also prevent him asking for clarification or help, which means he remains confused and becomes more anxious.

Executive function

Air traffic control resides in the control tower of an airport. Here, close attention is paid to the time management, prioritisation, sequencing and planning of the take-off and landing of all the aircraft. If there is an unexpected hitch to a landing, a new plan must be very rapidly formulated for that aircraft by the control tower staff. Airplanes are never allowed to take off or land just on impulse. This keeps the airport safe and effective each day and in all weathers.

In a very similar way neurotypical executive function, which resides in our frontal lobes, works as our control tower. Executive function manages the thoughts, words and actions we send out by using impulse control, time management, prioritisation, sequencing and planning. When executive function is weak, which may often be the case in young people on the autism spectrum, the ability to control impulses, manage time, prioritise, sequence and plan is impaired. For our young people, already experiencing a world where they cannot predict what will be said or might happen next, being impaired in how they sequence and plan their way through the social world adds to the confusion.

Literal language and negative language

Neurotypicals can instantly read the context of speech, so know when to take a phrase literally and when not to. Young people on the autism spectrum may not accurately read the context of speech, and therefore do not always understand the intended meaning; this can lead to a negative outcome for them. People around them may seem to never mean what they say, and this can be both incredibly frustrating and increasingly isolating.

Young people on the autism spectrum may also struggle to make sense of a negative command. A negative command, for example 'Don't run', requires the listener to recognise and use the context in order to make a good guess about what the teacher or parent may be wanting or expecting when they issue this negative command in this situation. This is a task our young people are less able to do well, if at all, due to both a lack of context sensitivity and a poor theory of mind. As a result of their non-compliance with a command, they may then be unfairly disciplined. Young people with autism need information and directions to be phrased positively in order for them to quickly and accurately understand the intended meaning. Simply rephrasing our comments using positive information can change our children's responses; for example, instead of 'Don't sit on the floor', say 'Sit on the chair, it's cleaner'.

A young person on the autism spectrum may both perceive and experience a great deal more negativity in their lives than their neurotypical peers and have a particularly negative outlook on life as a result. So it is only fair that this group of young people have access to all this missing social information presented to them in a completely accessible way. And that is where Social Stories™ can really help.

How Does a Social Story™ Help?

A Social Story™ shares missing social information. This information is missing because the child or adult has a different perspective of the world as a result of having a different way of processing the world around them. This means they may struggle to understand what the gist of a situation is, what is likely to be said next, what social language actually means, and what is likely to happen next and why. They may also be less aware of other people's feelings, thoughts and needs and therefore may be less able to take them into consideration in their interactions.

A Social Story therefore patiently and respectfully provides this information by describing the relevant clues in life, building and clarifying the context of a situation and providing a comforting sense of predictability. It shares other people's thoughts, feelings and experiences and links these to their reactions and expectations, thus explaining their behaviour. It does so in language that is always positive, literally accurate, and pitched at the exact cognitive level of the child or adult and therefore accessible to them. It works hard to engage the child or adult by considering their choice of interests and may include illustrations which highlight the content of the Story. The result is a uniquely meaningful, patient, non-judgemental, respectful and reassuring description of life.

To write a Social Story it is important to first abandon all assumptions, opinions or judgements of the child's response and work hard to try to understand the situation from the child or adult's perspective. Eject the thought 'I know he understands…'!

His perspective will lead to the missing information, and once this has been identified it can then be shared in the most accessible way for him. Carol Gray has defined ten criteria to guide safe and effective Social Story writing (Gray, 2015). Following them really helps the author to write a Story that is accessible, safe and effective for the individual person. When the criteria are not kept in mind it is easy to inadvertently stray into a story that just tells the child or adult what to do, rather than finding and sharing the actual social information they are missing. A guide to the criteria can be found in Carol Gray's recent book *The New Social Story Book* (2015) or on her website.[1]

I began to write Social Stories™ for my son, who was diagnosed as being on the autism spectrum when he was 3 years old. I have continued to write them throughout his life. He has grown up with Social Stories and is now 25 years old. I am still writing them today with continued success, and I fully expect to be writing them in some form into my old age.

---

1   www.carolgraysocialstories.com

Because the Stories are best crafted for each individual, they may be used across the spectrum for all ages and abilities, provided time is taken to research the child or adult's perspective and it is then written accordingly for the individual. My son's Stories have changed in format, illustration, vocabulary and detail as he has grown and developed in language and understanding over the years. This more adult format of Social Story is referred to as a Social Article. The examples of both Stories and Articles included in this book are taken from different points in his life and development, but focus mainly on his older adolescent and young adult years as we were able to bring together Stories around resilience in a more generalised form. This generalisation was planned and built by reusing a 'MasterStory' format for different contexts, culminating in a final Story using examples from previous Stories to enhance its meaning.

The illustrations were, and are, meaningful for him still today. Illustrations are as important as the text. The drawings I used were mostly taken from a Comic Strip Conversation (Gray, 1994) I would carry out with him to explore his perspective before writing the Story. Illustration within a Social Story must be chosen carefully to be literally accurate for the child or adult; in other words, the information must be clear from the picture without any contextual understanding being required. No distracting background detail is included. Early on, the Stories were illustrated with photographs because my son did not have symbolic understanding of drawn figures. As he developed this, and in fact became interested in anime, the illustrations changed with him. Every time I write a Social Story, I have to identify the best way to illustrate the text for that individual child, adolescent or adult. I have found that although higher functioning people do not usually want to see illustrations that look childlike in a Social Article, often if these are adapted for their higher level of understanding they can aid comprehension because the visual image is so powerful for them.

Social Stories and Social Articles are not a stand-alone strategy; they work well with many other positive concrete strategies to build social understanding. Some of the methods I found helpful have been included here in addition to the Stories which worked alongside them.

Fifty per cent of all Social Stories written for a child or adult should recognise and applaud his or her achievements, qualities and talents. Many people only reach for a Social Story when they encounter a social response that is unusual, usually after other strategies have been unhelpful. I have written a large number of successful Stories in response to a behaviour that demonstrated a misunderstanding or frustration in this way, for both my son and many others over the years. In my experience as a Social Stories trainer, once the missing information has been identified, and the Story shared, nine times out of ten the unusual response disappears as a direct result of the improved social understanding.

However, to just use this approach to target specific difficulties wastes another valuable and important use of Social Stories. This strategy can be used throughout an individual's life across the lifespan, each Story building on the last, continually developing concepts, and eventually becoming a truly unique description of life delivered in a crafted and meaningful way for that individual. In much the same way as a parent continually explains life to a neurotypical child as they grow, Social Stories allow the parent to do the same for an autistic child. This is why the Social Stories approach is such an incredibly useful strategy to use to develop resilience in our young people.

I was originally drawn to Carol Gray's strategy because of her phenomenal insight into the different, yet equally valid, perspective of autistic people. Underpinning all my writing and teaching today is my profound respect and admiration for all those who are on the autism spectrum and a strong belief that understanding their perspective of the world is fundamental to any successful intervention.

What is Resilience?

In 1991, during the Gulf War, Major Rhonda Cornum was the flight surgeon aboard a U.S. armed helicopter on a search and rescue mission when the helicopter was shot down and several of her team were killed. Badly wounded, she was captured and made a prisoner of war. Her ordeal lasted eight days before she was rescued. After recovering, Rhonda wrote about her experience (Cornum, 1992), sharing her resilient mind set which had helped her remain positive throughout the hugely traumatic experience and prevented her from developing any mental health consequences. She became renowned for this resilience, which she describes as partly innate in her character, but mostly learned through her upbringing.

In response to unprecedented levels of post-traumatic stress disorder, anxiety, depression and increasing suicide rates within the force, the U.S. military subsequently asked her, along with Martin Seligman and Michael Matthews, to develop and deliver a resilience training programme for their soldiers to prepare them for life in the forces in theatre and at home: the Comprehensive Soldiers Fitness Program (CSF). Central to this scheme was placing an equivalent amount of emphasis on resilience training as on physical fitness training. Rhonda is now an internationally acclaimed expert on resilience and positive psychology. It is her firm belief that people may be born with varying degrees of resilience but that anyone, of any age, can be trained to *improve* their resilience. She has shown that resilience can be taught, and she has successfully done so in the CSF (Harms *et al.*, 2013).

I became interested in her story long before my son's diagnosis, but her work on developing realistic optimism definitely influenced how I subsequently guided him and also how I approached being a parent of a young person with autism.

Resilience is the ability to bounce back from adversity, to weather the storms of life without slipping into despondency and depression. Resilient people are noted to be realistic optimists, seeing the positive side to any negative situation whilst acknowledging the difficulty facing them. They are usually flexible to change, and have the capability to self-reflect and empathise, as well as the support of a network of friends. All of these qualities are compromised for the young person with autism, who in contrast may have a tendency to focus and dwell on the negative events in his life.

There is currently a growing awareness and concern in the neurotypical world about the mental and emotional wellbeing of our young people with autism, with studies showing a high incidence of poor mental health within this group (Simonoff *et al.*, 2008). I share this concern, but it does not surprise me. I have always thought that the challenges faced by a young person with autism in a neurotypical world were so harsh and unremitting that they almost inevitably would lead to low self-esteem and subsequent depression at some point, unless active intervention occurs. I could clearly see that this group of people needed to be more resilient than their peers, and yet their different way of processing the world unfortunately rendered them much less resilient. I decided early on to try to help my son develop the best resilience he could have.

Resilience skills will need to be taught, practised, modelled and then supported if they are going to make a difference for a child or adult on the autism spectrum. As they do not come naturally, like many other things they will need to be repetitively rehearsed until they eventually become almost second nature. This is also true for neurotypicals learning resilience, but the process is comparatively quicker and easier for them.

The difference in how resilience may be taught to an individual child with autism is that it needs to be done in a way that is accessible and meaningful for him, in a language he fully understands and in a very concrete way, patiently building the concepts with improved understanding over time, and here Social Stories™ can really help.

It is generally accepted that healthy habits like practising mindfulness, regular exercise, sufficient sleep and a healthy diet also have an equally important contribution to mental wellbeing and resilience.

This book will focus on the strategies and the Social Stories I have written and used, and still use, to support the following five concepts and skills in my son. These skills are currently recognised by most people as being amongst those essential for developing good resilience.

- Positive thinking (building realistic optimism)
    - » being able to think about the positive side to every situation that arises
    - » noticing positive kind behaviour in other people and in oneself
    - » being conscious and mindful of the good things in life
    - » having a positive purpose in life
- Plan B (building flexibility to change)
    - » having plan B ready for when plan A is not working
    - » when no plan B is present, knowing who knows what plan B is and knowing to ask them
- Past successes (building positive self-reflection)
    - » being able to look back on how past challenges were overcome to give confidence in facing a new challenge
    - » being able to recall strategies that worked well in the past

- Personal best (building 'the best me I can be!')

  » recognising one's own talents and abilities

  » having realistic expectations of being the best I can be in any situation, with the talents and abilities I have

- Positive self-talk (building self-confidence)

  » using positive statements, based on fact and experience, to regain confidence and self-control in a situation.

Over time I described each skill area in Social Stories, using examples from real life that were meaningful for Mark. I then wrote the following Story to explain the purpose of learning resilience and to connect together the five skill areas we had been previously working on.

What is resilience?

Resilience is the ability to make the best of any situation. Some people are born with more resilience than others. Everyone's resilience may be improved with practice. Resilience is an important skill to try to improve because having resilience usually helps people feel more comfortable in any kind of situation.

Many people have found that resilience may be improved by working on the following five skills:

1. Learning to think in a **P**ositive way

2. Preparing a **P**lan B

3. Thinking about **P**ast successes

4. Using a **P**ersonal best strategy

5. Using **P**ositive self-talk.

I may think about these five skills as my five positive 'P's. The following Stories may help me develop the skills I need to become more resilient. Mum, Dad and my brothers will help me too. I am learning how to improve my resilience.

Chapter 1

Positive Thinking

Building Realistic Optimism

Lack of social and sporting success, and often also lack of academic success, may result in a negative daily school and work experience for the young person with autism. This may be compounded by a continual anxiety that comes from being unable to predict what may happen next, confusion over language, and a sensory dysregulation. Often this may be exacerbated by neurotypical adults misunderstanding the responses of the young person, leading to unfair discipline and sanctions.

The human brain is instinctively more tuned to negative happenings than positive, in order to take action to keep us safe and ensure survival. Frederickson describes in her book *Positivity* how neurotypicals need three positive experiences to every negative experience in order to flourish (Frederickson, 2010). I suspect that this ratio needs to be much higher for those with autism, in order to redress the balance, and therefore maintain reasonable mental wellbeing. Active intervention to increase positivity in every way possible is therefore needed.

Using a positive link phrase

To help my son, I began in his early childhood to consistently model a positive take on the small disappointments in day-to-day life. I was aiming to build a familiar framework and skill set, as a habit, so that when larger challenges arose later on in life this realistic yet optimistic way of thinking would kick in semi-automatically for him. I continued to do this in a consistent manner, despite not seeing any initial progress, and many years later I began to witness the development of a more positive balance in his interpretation of the disappointing situations he encounters on a day-to-day basis. His resilience is definitely improving. On occasions he is now even reminding me to 'look on the positive side'.

How did I go about this? Each time there was an unexpected situation that meant something Mark was looking forward to was cancelled, postponed or changed, I would remain very calm, while acknowledging and validating the disappointing feeling. Then, *in the same sentence*, I would describe a positive outcome that might happen instead, or something that might be learnt from the situation. I did this by linking both statements with what I called my positive phrase: '…but on the positive side…'

I continually tried to think of positive alternative things to suggest that interested Mark and would hold some attraction for him even in the face of a huge disappointment. I always used the literal, accurate and meaningful language that is so much part of the Social Story™ approach. I did not dismiss the disappointment, but instead tried to include it in a positive balancing statement. I think it is the idea of this balance that made Mark eventually choose the phrase 'in return' for his positive phrase, which is meaningful for him, and he now spontaneously uses this phrase in the way I have previously modelled for him. Another child may find the use of colour to represent the 'positive side' more useful. Parents and professionals need to find a link phrase that is meaningful for the young person they are working with. Care should be taken with phrases that are not literally meaningful, for example 'on the other hand'. In the Stories included here I have continued to use 'on the positive side' as the positive link phrase.

A good example of how I used this positive link phrase to consider both the negative and positive in the same sentence occurred when the swimming pool was closed unexpectedly and Mark's regular swimming lesson was cancelled. We discovered this only when we arrived at the door to the pool. I quickly modelled a positive response by describing what might happen instead of a swimming lesson by saying, 'This is *very* disappointing, *but on the positive side* you will have more time for gaming before tea.' He began to think about this possible positive outcome and started to settle even though he was hugely upset. Because this had clearly worked, I wrote a short Social Story about it later that evening so we could reflect on it again and again. By stating what was disappointing and then linking that with a positive outcome, I was demonstrating that there is always something positive to find even in a challenging disappointment.

Another example was when a meet-up with friends to play Yu-gi-oh cards was cancelled at the last minute. Mark was very disappointed. I thought quickly and said, 'This is *really* disappointing, *but on the positive side* you will have more time to prepare an even better deck of cards before the next meet-up.' I knew that building a great set of cards in a deck was important to Mark and could help him do better at the game, but it did take time to do. Although upset, he could see that this was a possible positive outcome and again settled quickly. I wrote a Social Story about it.

A much more up-to-date and recent example happened when Mark's driving instructor was changed unexpectedly without warning by the driving centre. I was expecting him to have a great deal of anxiety and possibly refuse to drive as a result. I remained calm, which was difficult, and reflected on how surprising and unexpected this had been: 'Well, that is a surprise, which is very uncomfy, *but on the positive side* maybe you may learn something new from this instructor.'

Mark agreed to have his lesson and afterwards told his dad that although it had been a surprise which was *definitely* uncomfy, 'in return' he had learnt how to change gear without looking at the gearstick, which was a new skill. This was the first time I heard him use his own positive phrase.

Balancing the positive qualities of autism against challenges

Once Mark had been introduced to his diagnosis using a Social Story entitled 'What are worries?' (Timmins, 2016), he began to ask questions about the challenges he experienced and whether they were attributable to his autism. I never let this sort of situation pass without emphasising the positive side to his autistic response. I was determined to give him a balanced view of his many qualities and talents when addressing his difficulties and challenges. For example, when frustrated that he could not tolerate a dead pixel on a screen, he asked me whether this was because of his autism. 'Yes,' I replied, 'your autism means you notice tiny details that others cannot see. In this situation it is frustrating, *but on the positive side* you may be able to locate and fix errors in computer screens in the workplace in the future.'

Another example was when he found it difficult to transition from one task to the next. He asked again if this was due to his autism. 'Yes,' I replied, 'your autism means you have terrific focus. In this situation this means that moving from task to task is difficult, *but on the positive side* once involved in a task you are so focused you get it done to a high standard without being distracted. This is a skill many employers want in their employees.'

Constantly identifying the good in every difficult situation and commenting on it positively reframes his perspective. It helps me too!

Noticing the positive and being thankful

There were other ways I helped my son towards a more positive outlook. Noticing the kind things that others do for us and commenting on them makes them feel good and cheers us up too, as we become more tuned in to the good things happening around us. I taught Mark to use the phrase 'Thank you, that was very kind of you' when someone helped him or gave him a present. He learned to write it in his 'thank you' letters too and eventually began to use it without prompting. This simple phrase stimulated such a visually positive response from others that it was easy to describe and illustrate in a Social Story how good other people felt when they heard it. Saying it out loud each time he thanked people reinforced the concept for him.

To focus him on his own positive talents and qualities I constructed a book of pictures that clearly and concretely demonstrated these and asked other important people in his life to also contribute. Each picture was a drawing showing him engaged in an activity that demonstrated one of his talents, for example surfing and playing computer games, or in an event which showed one of his qualities, for example bravery – he once saved a parked car from rolling downhill as a passenger by applying the handbrake, and a picture showed this event![1]

---

1   I used the format described by Carol Gray in the workbook *Pictures of Me*. This is still available to download, free of charge, from Carol Gray's website (www.carolgraysocialstories.com/articles-newsletters/the-morning-newsjenison-autism-journal) under 'The Morning News' (Fall '96, pp.9–15).

I have always reflected on my own day before sleeping and tried to recall the good things that have happened, feeling grateful for each one. Counting blessings or completing a gratitude journal leads to a growing awareness of the good things that are often forgotten or unnoticed in life. To be thankful for positive things in life though, we have to train ourselves initially to notice them and then to recall them. Reflection and recall, particularly around social events in the day, is difficult for young people on the autism spectrum. They may need help to do so. Looking at nature with an artist's eye by focusing on colour, shape and light is an excellent way of letting nature reassure us of the beauty in the world, even on a difficult or challenging day. Noticing and drawing Mark's attention to a small detail that is beautiful, such as a rainbow in a puddle, helped him focus on positive details in his surroundings. Some children with autism become talented photographers using their detail-sensitive eye to produce photographs that demonstrate a different perspective on life. I tried to notice things that he would find interesting and unusual but which were also beautiful and drew his attention to them. I learnt how to choose my objects carefully so that he would engage with them. Nowadays Mark is extremely knowledgeable about different dog breeds, so we frequently draw each other's attention to different breeds of dogs we see as we walk or drive about, commenting on the different shapes and attributes of each dog, and the individual beauty of their appearance.

Positive affirmation

Following the description of Mark's unique qualities and talents, I wrote a short Social Story titled 'Who loves me?' (see later in the chapter). This described who loved him and was the simplest affirmation of positive elements in his life. Knowing who loves you is not a given for those on the autism spectrum because they are not continually mindful of what others are feeling or thinking. I emphasised this with thought bubbles containing the words 'I love Mark' coming from each person featured in the Story. Later on I developed the concept, explaining what 'believing' in someone meant. I used the now familiar format and titled it 'Who believes in me?' (see later in the chapter). This explained that when someone says they 'believe in' a person this means that they know and have confidence in the person's qualities and talents. This developed the positive idea that there were people who believed in him and valued him *just as he is*.

These Stories were not written reactively to address a behaviour or response that displayed a lack of understanding; they were written *proactively* to build my son's positivity bank with concrete positive information about what others feel, know and believe – information that is just 'there' for neurotypicals but may be absent for someone who does not possess theory of mind. These Stories are short and very positive, and made both of us feel better after reading them. They still do, so I have included both Stories in this chapter as examples.

Reframing perspective from negative to positive

Being mindful of all the things that are good and right in our lives helps us put the more negative things in proper perspective. As a family, when we sat down to eat each evening we would ask each other at the dinner table what each other's day had been like. To do so we used the question 'What was good about your day today?' rather than 'How was your day?', which can be more confusing for a literal person. For children on the autism spectrum, recalling the good bits in the day is difficult as they tend to focus on the injustices. They may need help in directing themselves to a positive experience. With consistent patient modelling by everyone at the table, and with daily repetition, eventually Mark began to try and think of something good that happened in his day in response to the question 'What was good about your day today?', and later on even began to ask the question first himself when he met family, eventually even using the question 'How was your day?'.

To balance perspective at the end of a school day, we would sometimes colour in periods of the day that had been okay or good on a paper copy of his timetable. This allowed him to concretely see that often, even on a day that had a particularly disastrous lesson, there were good and even great times too. The predominant overall colour then led to the description of the 'kind' of day it had been.

Mark's experience at school was an overall good one, due to close co-operation between home and school and his wonderful Learning Support Assistant (LSA). He had some fabulous teachers too! But sometimes he would have a difficult day despite everyone's efforts. On these occasions we would count the total hours spent at school and compare it to the total number spent at home. This is a surprising exercise. The child's school day may begin at 9 am and finish at 3.30 pm, which is a total of six-and-a-half hours. By the time he goes to bed the child will have spent two hours before school and at least four hours after school away from school on any normal day. He may then also spend a further 8 to 10 hours asleep at home, which brings a total home time of between 14 and 16 hours. Even if he does not sleep well, these are still hours that are spent at home. When this is coloured in on a bar chart or pie chart it is clear where the majority of his time is spent, and if he has been relatively comfortable in that time then the majority of the day has been okay. Of course, this will not take away the difficulties and disappointments experienced by the child. It doesn't intend to – it just seeks to demonstrate the positive times in an attempt to rebalance the perspective.

This calculation can be extended to depict how much time is spent at school over the course of a week or even a year. When holidays and weekends are taken into account, school begins to fade into the background in terms of time spent there. For older students struggling within the education system, this technique can concretely show them that, taking a long-term view, education may take 11 years of life compared to a whole lifespan of 80-plus years. It is not a forever place! This strategy is also a useful way of helping some young people who recognise that they are more successful socially with adults than their peers.

Demonstrating to them concretely that in their lifetime they will spend 60 or more years working and living with adults and only 11 years working with students of a similar age can help reassure them that there is something to look forward to in the future! Of course, it goes without saying that for these students all efforts should also be made to help them in their current situation, this strategy being an additional one to other strategies, including Social Stories™, which improve social understanding.

A group of friends, or even one reliable friend, can be a powerful ally when faced with a setback. A friend can help a young person feel valued and encouraged and therefore help recovery from a negative experience. Fully understanding what other people need or think also helps a young person formulate a plan B when in a tough or challenging situation (Siebert, 2005). Having empathy and developing friendship is therefore important in developing resilience.

Unfortunately, young people on the autism spectrum, as a result of poor theory of mind, usually have a reduced or absent friendship group and therefore miss out on this valuable 'rebalancing' benefit. They are also less able to read others' intentions, which leads to a tendency to blame others, or interpret the actions of others as deliberately malevolent. This personalises the setback, which then prevents them moving towards a solution. Without peer friendship to raise their diminishing self-worth, they may sink into a sea of negativity.

Social Stories and Social Articles can provide the missing information about what another person is thinking or feeling, which is vital for developing empathy. They help with understanding others' intentions too (Timmins, 2017). They may also gently coach the young person to an alternative response to ease social interactions and help friendship along. Social Stories around friendship, combined with Comic Strip Conversation (Gray, 1994), are invaluable in building an understanding of the thoughts, feelings and intentions of others, and bringing a more positive balance to a young person's outlook.

Positive purpose in life

Having a positive purpose in life builds up our bank of positivity. We all like to feel that our presence in the world is noticed and makes a difference, giving us a reason for being alive. For neurotypicals this partly comes from our role in the workplace, doing a good job and working well towards a goal as part of a team. Affirmation may come from a line manager, supervisor or colleagues. It also comes from being part of a group of friends and from family membership too.

For those on the autism spectrum work may be elusive, and therefore there is a need to find activities that make a difference to others, not solely to benefit others, but also to build for the young person a positive understanding of his value in the world. Many of our young people feel on the edges of society, have few positive outcomes from their interactions and therefore may sometimes feel that no one would even notice if they weren't there. It is important then to continually work on ways that they can contribute in their own way to the general good, and then comment on that using a concrete, positive Social Story. This allows the young person time to think about the content, to be able to read it over and over and make it a tangible part of their history, something they can come back to whenever they wish.

As socialising is such a challenge, a shorter working day may help the young person manage their anxieties, and many benefit from part-time work to make it accessible and possible. Volunteering and work experience can also be helpful to allow access to the workplace, building self-esteem.

When it is visually very clear that another person is in distress with poverty, homelessness or starvation, it is easier for our young people to have empathy and want to help that person. They frequently want to challenge injustice in the world, and may even be moved to do it themselves, sometimes placing themselves at risk. Encouraging helping others in a safe and practical way is important. Instead of opening a wallet on the street to give money to a homeless person, the young adult may be encouraged to make a regular habit of clearing and donating unused possessions to a charity that directly provides shelter, warmth, food and clothing for the homeless. Raising money for charities is also another way to regularly do something good for an appreciative group and give purpose to life. Charities are usually very happy to provide 'thank you' letters on receipt of donations, which are concrete and permanent reminders of having made a difference in the world. These then can be included as part of the resource along with the Social Story or Social Article.

Many young people on the autism spectrum develop very positive and rewarding relationships with animals, particularly dogs, cats and horses. An animal does not ask questions, is consistently loving towards them, always is pleased to see them and does not have a bewildering array of facial expressions and body language to decipher. Love is unconditional with a pet animal. If having an animal of his own is not possible, having access to a therapy dog or horse can be very helpful, and volunteering at dog and cat rescue centres can provide this important link.

Developing a special interest around a common type of pet can be very helpful when meeting new people as it is a useful link into neurotypical conversation. I was absolutely delighted when my son started to develop a special interest in different dog breeds!

Mark subsequently developed a very close relationship with our family dog, Rosie. Each week for the past five years he has brought Rosie to dog training classes. He has a one-to-one session with the trainer, guiding him and Rosie in dog agility and dog tricks. The sessions encourage her obedience and make 'work' for her active terrier's working brain! She now responds to Mark more readily than other members of the family. He can ask her to do things for him that others cannot and he has amassed a set of certificates of achievement in the process.

Being needed by another person or animal gives a positive purpose to life. Rosie needs Mark to interact with her, not just to feed her and walk her. Mark helps and reassures Rosie just as much as she helps and reassures him. It is a true friendship and partnership. I wrote the Social Story 'Rosie and me' (see later in the chapter) to describe this relationship, and when I read it I was immediately struck by how much information it contained about *all* friendships.

Positive communication

To build a more positive experience in life we need to be aware of how we communicate with our children. The child with autism may not take the same meaning from negative directions as neurotypicals. This is because when an adult tells a child *not* to do something the child must be able to quickly make a guess about what the adult wants him *to do* instead, in this particular context. For the child on the autism spectrum, recognising and using the context may be difficult, and his ability to guess the thoughts of another person may be impaired. There is a simple solution: give positive instructions, not negative ones! This has two positive effects – first, the child has a positive experience, because he is now able to comply with what is asked of him and he may receive praise for doing so. Second, the adult, who has been constantly saying 'Don't…!', which is a draining and negative experience, finds relief in the child's improved response to positive directions and therefore also has a positive experience.

Social Stories use positive language and always avoid negative vocabulary. A Social Story will never describe a negative behaviour or response in the first person. Positive communication is an important part of writing Social Stories. Choosing positive communication over negative instruction is a very effective way to share social information and to build positivity.

Positive comments

As children grow older, both parents and teachers stop telling them everything they are doing well and start only commenting usually when their work needs amending or correcting. The neurotypical child can guess what the adult may be thinking and knows that when the adult is not correcting them he or she is likely to be happy with what they are doing. The child with autism may struggle to think what the adult may be thinking and therefore may not realise that he or she is happy with his efforts unless the adult says so. Praise Social Stories and Praise Comments, are an extremely effective way to let the child know that what they are doing is correct and praiseworthy (Timmins, 2017). Making this praise very specific and succinct prevents it being interpreted as patronising.

Praise Social Stories or Social Articles are written about a talent or quality the child has, or about something they have achieved or done well. Praise Comments (Timmins, 2017) are positive comments that are recorded in a book along with the name of the person who makes them, and the date, time and place of the comment. The concrete accessibility and permanence of this record means it can be referred to again and again in a way that quickly boosts self-esteem.

The more I work on improving Mark's positivity and resilience, the more I notice my own positivity and resilience grows. Reading and reflecting on positive comments others have made about my son readjusts my perspective too, and builds up my positivity and energy. The parent of a young person with autism also needs to be resilient and resourceful in order to help their child and continue to look after the rest of the family as well as themselves over a lifetime. We can all benefit from improving our resilience!

The following Social Stories describe learning to think in a positive way. The first is an example of one situation where learning to think in a positive way was used successfully and this was written after the event. The second pulls together the concept of positive thinking referring to the previous Story, and another, as examples.

The third Story included here is 'Rosie and me', describing Mark's relationship with his dog. The fourth Story describes 'Who loves me?', and this is followed by 'Who believes in me?'

Beginning to think in a positive way

Most of the time good things happen. Sometimes disappointing things happen. This is how life happens for all adults and children.

Yesterday many good things happened and one disappointing thing happened. I got a certificate at assembly, I enjoyed my Art lesson and I played a game at break time. These were all good positive things to happen.

After school my swimming lesson was cancelled. This was very disappointing.

Mum helped me think about what good things could happen instead of my swimming lesson. I used my positive phrase to think, 'I am disappointed, **but on the positive side** I have more time to play games before tea.'

I played my game before tea and went up a level. It was disappointing to have a lesson cancelled, **but on the positive side** I enjoyed playing my game.

I am beginning to think in a positive way about disappointing events.

Learning to think in a positive way

Most of the time good things happen. Sometimes disappointing things happen. This is how life happens for all adults and children. Learning to think about things that happen in life in a positive way usually helps people feel happier.

There is usually something positive in every situation. I am learning to think about disappointing situations in a positive way. To do this I may think about what positive things may happen instead or I may think about what I may learn from the situation. Thinking in a positive way is sometimes called 'looking on the positive side'.

A positive phrase may help me to think about a situation in a positive way. One positive phrase is '...*but on the positive side*...' Mum sometimes uses this phrase to help her think about what is positive in a disappointing situation. I may use this phrase too or I may choose another one. This is okay.

Two weeks ago, my swimming lesson was cancelled. I was disappointed but I thought about what good things may happen instead. I used my positive phrase to think, 'I am disappointed, **but on the positive side** I have more time to play games before tea.'

Last Saturday I was expecting to meet my friends to play Yu-gi-oh but the day was cancelled. I was disappointed but I used my positive phrase to think, 'This is disappointing, **but on the positive side** I have more time to improve my deck before we next meet up.'

Sometimes it is easy to think what the positive side is, sometimes it is tricky. When it is tricky Mum knows how to help me. Thinking in a positive way needs practice. With practice it usually becomes easier to do.

I am learning to use my positive phrase to think about things in a positive way.

Rosie and me

My dog Rosie is a Parson Russell terrier. She is 11 years old.

I enjoy talking to Rosie and playing with her. Rosie enjoys being with me and playing with me.

I feel comfortable and safe with Rosie and she feels comfortable and safe with me. Rosie loves me and I love her. Rosie always tries to make me happy. She helps me feel better when I feel sad. I try to make Rosie happy too.

Rosie is important to me. I am important to Rosie too. Because she is important to me I spend time with her, walking her and training her. Once a week we go to dog training classes together to learn new tricks with our instructor.

Most days we have a walk together before I go into work. This usually helps me feel calm and helps Rosie feel calm too. We help each other.

When I go to work Rosie usually goes
home with Mum. Rosie is always pleased
to see me when I get home after work
and I am always pleased to see Rosie.

I am the luckiest owner in the world
because I have Rosie. Rosie is the luckiest
dog in the world because she has me. We
are friends and partners in an awesome
team. We have certificates and rosettes
to prove it!

Who loves me?

I have a family who love me. This is a picture of some of my family.

My mum loves me.

My dad loves me.

My brothers love me.

My grannies and granddads love me.

My dog Rosie loves me.

I have a family and a dog who all love me.

I love my family and my dog too.

Who believes in me?

Thinking about who believes in me usually helps me think more positively. When a person believes in someone it usually means that they know and have confidence in that person's qualities and talents. Many people know and have confidence in my qualities and talents. Many people believe in me.

I have a family who love me and believe in me.

I have a wonderful dog Rosie who loves me and believes in me.

I have work colleagues and friends who like me and believe in me. My boss at work likes me and believes in me.

I will try to remember who believes in me to help me think more positively.

Chapter 2

Plan B

Building Flexibility to Change

As neurotypicals we are able to get the gist or context of a situation very quickly and without any conscious thought. We use the context or 'gist' to help us focus only on the relevant social clues in a situation that tell us what has happened already, and what is happening now, ignoring all irrelevant clues. This allows us to work out what is likely to happen next and what behaviour and language might be safe and effective to employ. We are able to do this because we have context sensitivity and central coherence working well for us. Understanding a rapidly and continually changing context allows us to be flexible, adapting to each situation we find ourselves in as it comes along.

Children and adults on the autism spectrum do not have these processes working so well for them, so they struggle to recognise and use a context to predict what might be said next or what might happen next. They may therefore choose a behaviour or language that is unsafe or ineffective in this context as a result.

Consequently they are constantly on a mission to find clarity and predictability. They find change extremely difficult and may always strive to keep things the same. When a timetable is suddenly altered or a plan derailed, they may become very upset. In addition, their executive functioning may be weak. This means that their planning, sequencing and prioritising skills may not be working well for them. When plan A fails they will try plan A over and over, harder and harder. They may be unable to come up with a plan B on the spot. This may lead to huge frustration, as they frequently try to solve every situation themselves rather than ask for help. Not asking for help is often the result of not being mindful that other people have other ideas or experiences that might help solve a problem they are experiencing; this is due to poor theory of mind.

Sharing social understanding with the child with autism builds flexibility. Social Stories™ do this by describing the specific information that the child is missing, filling in what others think and feel and why, and describing what the context of a situation is and how it may change. A Social Story™ may include a gentle guide towards a safe and effective response too. I have found over the last 22 years that describing life with Social Stories improves flexibility in the long term as well as in the immediate situation. It seems it is the lack of social information that often leads to the inflexible behaviour of a child with autism. Once provided with this information, the child may become surprisingly flexible.

When faced with a plan A that is not working, neurotypicals are able to very rapidly formulate a plan B by using their understanding of the ever-changing surrounding context and their executive functioning skills. Our children with autism, on the other hand, may have to *consciously* think through a changing context and its implications, which is inevitably a much slower process.

Spending time consciously developing a plan B strategy at the outset using Social Stories and real life modelling can result in quite a dramatic improvement in flexibility to deal with unexpected disappointment. This requires a lot of adult help. Whenever Mark and I planned an outing, chose a present, organised a game or even decided what we were going to do for the day at home, we called it our plan A. Then we always tried to put together a plan B before we started plan A. Plan B was our second-best idea. Introducing this at the outset really helped when plan A went wrong because now when plan B was put into action it was familiar and expected. Mark accepted it much better than if we had tried to formulate an alternative in the midst of the distress of disappointment. Having a plan B helps *prepare for disappointment* and brings a sense of predictability.

Life is full of unexpected events and it takes time and effort to think through an effective plan B solution 'on the hoof'. I spent an evening writing down several things that Mark liked to do so that I could bring one to mind quickly when a disappointing situation arose. These were going to be put in place instead of the expected event, so they needed to be things that he would be really happy to engage with.

Initially, Mark would refuse to consider a plan B. Over time, as it became a familiar habit, he began to accept this way of doing things and now, years later, is happy to make a plan B for himself.

An example of a plan B might be a different colour case on a game console that has been put on a Christmas present list (in case the first-choice colour is unavailable), or a plan for an activity that the child enjoys indoors in case it rains during a trip to the beach.

If the child does not have a plan B, it is a good idea to talk to him about people who might know a plan B, such as his LSA for example. Knowing that someone knows the plan, and will tell the child, can alleviate the awful anxiety of just not knowing what is going to happen next.

I would write a Social Story describing plan A and plan B whenever I could, and I would talk about it too so that the idea became commonplace. Each time a plan B had to be put into place, and upset decreased or avoided, I wrote a simple Social Story describing what had happened and how plan B had helped. After a while I was able to write a Story which described how having a plan B helped in *general*, bringing the concept together with examples of previous Stories included within it.

The first Story in this chapter is 'Today we are going to the zoo', which was an early and simple Social Story, explaining plan A and plan B for a zoo visit. The second Story demonstrates how the concept was built upon and developed.

Mark now frequently makes his own plan B without any prompting.

Today we are going to the zoo

Today Mum and I are going to the zoo. The zoo has meerkats and penguins and lots of other animals. The zoo has an indoor ball pond.

Mum and I have made a plan to see the meerkats and the penguins. This is our best plan. We call it plan A.

If it rains we will go to the indoor ball
pond. This is our second-best plan. We
call it plan B.

Mum and I are going to the zoo today
and we have a plan A and a plan B.

What is plan B?

Usually I have a plan of how I expect the day to be. Mum and I call this plan A. Plan A is our best plan for the day. Sometimes unexpected things happen to a plan. Having a plan B may help when unexpected things happen to plan A.

Plan B may be my second-best choice. Sometimes I decide on plan B when I make my plan A.

For example, I wanted a blue Nintendo 3DS™ for my Christmas present. This was my plan A present. I made a plan B choice too. My plan B choice was a black 3DS™. When the blue 3DS™ was sold out I was very disappointed, but I knew that I could have my plan B choice instead. I enjoyed playing on my black 3DS™.

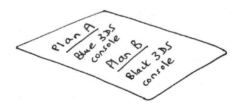

Another example was when we planned to go to the beach for the day. This was our plan A. We made a plan B choice too. Our plan B choice was that if it rained we would have fish and chips in the beach hut. When it rained I was disappointed that plan A was cancelled but I knew what would happen next and enjoyed my fish and chips in the beach hut.

Sometimes I have only made a plan A.
When something unexpected happens
to plan A, Mum, Mrs B. or another adult
usually knows what plan B is. When Plan
A is cancelled because of an unexpected
event I may ask what plan B is.

Having a plan B may help when
unexpected things happen to plan A. I am
learning about having a plan B.

Chapter 3

Past Successes

Building Positive Self-Reflection

Children with autism often struggle to identify social context and the key social events in the present and in the past. This may make it difficult to recall what happened in a day. When a parent asks them how school was, they may be unable to recall the key events in the order in which they happened. They may not even have noticed these social events due to weakness in their central coherence. Instead they were perhaps focusing on the things around them that were interesting to them, and these may not have been relevant to the social context of the situation they were in. So when asked 'How was your day?', they may reply, 'Dunno.' This may be frustrating for a parent who, desperate to hear that the child wasn't unhappy all day, then quizzes the child on all the possible problem areas. 'Who did you play with at playtime?', 'How did the Maths test go?', 'Who did you sit next to at lunch?', 'Did you talk to them?', 'Did you play any games at lunchtime?' This is natural for the parent to do, but hard for the child who may feel overwhelmed by the questions. Many parents like myself have eventually discovered that a completely calm, accepting, no-questions-asked welcome home is the best kind for their child at the end of a stressful day. Easier to say than do, I know.

Our children may find it difficult to self-reflect and think about what they have experienced in the past as they struggle to understand their own mind as well as that of others (Attwood, 2008). Episodic and autobiographical memory also works less well for them (Bowler, Gardiner and Grice, 2000; Goddard *et al.*, 2014). We use our autobiographical memory to give us a sense of self-identity and our life progress. We retrieve happy memories to cheer ourselves up and we hope for more of them in the future. We prepare for new challenges by reflecting on how we managed similar ones in the past. This gives us confidence, from which grows courage and perseverance. For the child with autism there may be comparatively fewer achievements in their past, but there will definitely always be some, and these need to be highlighted in a concrete way, and conscious efforts made to think about them. The construction of an 'Achievements' or 'Happiness' book to archive any achievement during the course of their life, whether it is a certificate or a photo of them performing a new skill which can be stuck in the book for reference, can really help here.

Many parents are already doing this, as collecting accolades is a natural thing to do for parents! This is a wonderful concrete way of building self-esteem and encouraging self-reflection. To aid the child in their self-reflection, however, maybe we need to go a little further.

Along the way, apart from positive achievements, such as swimming badges, house point certificates, etc., the child will have had to face what to others is the mundane stuff of life. To a child with autism this may be challenging. Some of it may reasonably be avoided, but some of it has to be got through in the most comfortable, safe and effective way possible. It is the successful navigation of previous challenges that builds confidence to try the next one, and this builds resilience. These mundane situations that pose difficulties for our children are rarely recorded in an album.

One example of a challenge Mark and many others face is the anxiety caused by trying something new. This was initially tackled with the Social Story™ 'How to discover another favourite food' (Timmins, 2016) with great success, and the format of this Story was used again and again to encourage tackling other new things. Trying a new sport was another challenge where I successfully applied the same format. Exercise and sport are very important for good physical health in life. Participating in a sport and belonging to a sports club also allows socialising *with a common interest*, and this is helpful for those on the autism spectrum, particularly as young adults after schooldays. Our young people, however, have a deep fear of change and new activities and situations. The Social Story 'Discovering another favourite game or sport' is included later in this chapter.

Another example of a mundane situation was when Mark had to manage a particularly long day at college on Fridays. This was not onerous for his peers because they were neurotypical, but the sheer length of the day sometimes without support was a huge struggle for Mark. There was no flexibility for a reduced length of day, so he had to navigate the whole day and needed a strategy to help him not to feel overwhelmed. We developed a simple method of breaking the day into three sections and thinking of it one section at a time. Offloading the morning's concerns at lunchtime allowed him to 'reset'. The word 'reset' chimed with his interest in computers. Reflection on this simple technique described in a Social Story helped when he faced another 'long day' challenge. The Story was written after the event for future reference. He was therefore able to reflect, with concrete support, on how he had tackled a difficult challenge and successfully overcome it. Knowing that we have overcome challenges in the past builds confidence when facing future changes. The long-day Story is included at the end of the chapter, titled 'Challenges I have overcome: The long-day Friday'.

It is clear that if a child cannot naturally recall having got through challenges before, then we need to help them to do so. Social Stories™ can do this extremely well. They share this missing information in a positive way that is concrete, meaningful, accessible, engaging and reassuring for the child with autism. A Social Story can effectively combine the description of a challenge overcome in the past with a description of overcoming a current challenge, leading to a prediction of the likelihood of overcoming a challenge in the future, based on factual past evidence! Collecting together Stories praising the child for achievements and accolades, as well as for challenges 'got through', can be collectively named as a 'past success' book.

This places getting through a challenging situation on the same achievement level as a certificate gained for a skill learned. This acknowledges the difficulty experienced in overcoming the challenge, and reinforces the positive outcome of employing a successful thinking strategy. Regular repeated review of this collection of Stories may help the child to learn, or at least improve, in a very conscious way, the skill of self-reflection and the concept of 'I have done it before, I can do it again', as well as giving them a bank of concrete strategies to put in place when another challenge comes along. To reinforce this, pictures or photos on the child's bedroom wall can be a visual reminder of a challenge successfully overcome, or an achievement, which can instantly boost self-esteem each day.

Discovering another favourite game or sport

My name is Mark. When I was a young child I played chasing games. Chasing games were my favourite game.

When I was older I tried football and discovered that I liked being a goalie. I was a good goalie. Football was another favourite game.

Then I tried swimming. I discovered that I liked swimming. I learned to swim. Swimming was another favourite game.

When I was older I tried fencing. I discovered that fencing was great fun. I learned how to fence and then I joined a fencing club. Now fencing is my most favourite game.

Trying new games and sports is a good way to discover favourite games or sports. Many children and adults have more than one favourite sport. Having many favourite sports helps keep the body healthy and working well.

I will work on trying another sport. I may decide I like it. I may decide I dislike it. This is okay. I may make an important discovery and find another favourite sport!

Challenges I have overcome:
The long-day Friday

I have been a baby, a toddler, a child
and adolescent. I am now a young adult.
I have learned many skills and achieved
many goals as I have grown up. These
skills and achievements are archived in
my 'Happiness' book. I am very proud
of them. My mum and dad are very
proud of these achievements too. Looking
at this book usually makes Mum, Dad and
me feel good.

Sometimes it is also helpful to think about
challenges I have overcome. Thinking
about how I got through a challenge may
remind me of strategies that work for
me. Thinking about how I got through
a challenge may remind me of what I
can do. This may help me when I meet
new challenges.

For example, last year at college
each Friday I had a long day from

9 am to 5 pm. Sometimes my LSA was
absent on Fridays. On Thursday evenings
I was usually anxious about the Friday.
Mum and I made a plan to make me as
comfortable as possible.

I thought about my Friday timetable in
two halves. I thought about the first half
of Friday until lunchtime. When the first
half was finished I met Mum for lunch at
the Noodle bar. I told Mum about the first
half. This helped me reset. After lunch I
thought about the second half of Friday.
Then I went and completed the second
half. Dividing the day into two halves and
thinking about one half at a time helped
me. I managed to do a long-day Friday
for a whole year, which was 36 Fridays in
total. Managing to do 36 long-day
Fridays is evidence that I overcame an
uncomfortable challenge. Next time I
have a long-day challenge I will try to
remember how I overcame my long-day
Friday challenge at college.

I am learning about overcoming challenges.

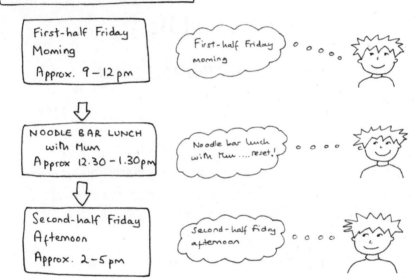

Chapter 4

Personal Best

Building 'The Best Me I Can Be'

Many young and old people on the autism spectrum struggle with winning and losing, often giving up at a new skill if they are not quickly successful. There may be many reasons for this, as set out below.

The child that crosses the finishing line first in a race is greeted by applause from spectators and congratulations from fellow competitors. The coach or teacher cheers him with a phrase such as 'Well done!' He is then awarded a cup, a medal, a ribbon or a certificate. This is a strong visual picture of success, attention and being appreciated. Many children and young adults on the autism spectrum perceive these strong visual images as being synonymous with friendship and popularity. Due to social isolation, some may crave friendship, belonging and being noticed as a worthwhile person. Being first, or the winner, may seem a powerful solution. Without theory of mind working well for the young person, he may be unaware of the feelings of others in the competitive situation. He may not realise that others want to win too, and are also disappointed when they lose. This can lead to a feeling of injustice when he loses and someone else wins, and a frustrated or angry response.

Being first in the line or queue is another kind of 'winning/losing' situation. Our young people frequently struggle when they are not first. Being first means that there is no waiting needed for a turn. Waiting is difficult to do without the social understanding that comes with theory of mind. There is also a clear status in being first in line and being acknowledged as the leader – the opposite of the anonymous state of being the outsider. There are sensory advantages too: the leader does not have someone in close proximity in front of him.

The way sports and games are introduced to children in school and at home may influence how the outcome is perceived. This usually begins with a definition of the objective of the sport or game – how to win. For the a-contextual, literal child there is little or no information at the outset about the progress that comes with practice of the skills of the sport or game. This is assumed but unspoken knowledge. When the child with autism fails to win, he may be devastated. Telling him, at this point, that 'taking part is fun', when he has failed the original objective set out at the start, makes no logical sense to him. Taking part is only fun if you have a sense of self-worth, with a knowledge that all children have different talents and that you have talents too. For some, talents lie in physical ability and they immediately succeed at a sport; for others, talents lie elsewhere. This is information that may not be available for the young person on the autism spectrum.

It is possible to help here. First, developing an understanding of his own talents and abilities and that of others is important. Second, giving a clear and accessible introduction is only fair. Being realistic about being a *beginner* at a sport, skill or academic subject allows an achievable expectation and allows a progression of skills with practice, gradually improving along the way. Many great players are not winners from the off but develop their skill through practice and training, with frequent failures on the way, and concrete examples of this can be described and referred to. Third, I have found that developing an understanding of the concept of 'personal best' has been a really effective way of helping many children deal with losing. It is also important in building resilience to failure in general. To begin with, I usually describe how the most important thing in sport, academic work and life is to try to improve to become the best you can be at whatever you are doing. Being the best one can be at something, and achieving a personal best, is the essence of optimistic realism. Recording a personal best score in a 'personal best' book each time a test, race or match takes place provides concrete visual evidence of achievement over time, which encourages continued effort and participation. Aiming for a personal best makes taking part more fun. Of course, sometimes results do not improve by even a point, and in these situations, the average scores over a period of time can be used to evidence improvement.

The Personal Best Social Story™ was originally written for my son because of the competitive element within school sports. The one included in this chapter was written years later following the familiar format. The sentence length is longer, the font smaller, and the vocabulary more advanced than in the previous Stories. It is therefore referred to as a Social Article. Every Social Story or Social Article must be written for the individual young person with respect to their cognitive level.

The personal best concept can be applied to all kinds of activities, from sport to academic tests to learning musical instruments, or even the time it takes to get dressed. It was helpful again years after leaving school when Mark learned to fence and joined a fencing club. As a novice amongst experienced fencers, some who had been fencing for over 25 years, Mark was unlikely to win a match on club night for some time. To prevent him becoming disheartened, I introduced the 'personal best' book again with immediate success. This has allowed him to develop into the good fencer he is today and to be part of an adult social club, while continuing to build his resilience along the way.

What is my personal best?

Fencing club night usually happens on Monday and Friday evenings. On club night, members fence other club members.

Some members have been fencing for many years and are highly skilled and experienced fencers. There are a few beginners at the club. By fencing more experienced fencers the beginners practise the moves they have been taught in their coaching lessons. This is usually how fencers improve their skill at the sport.

Before each match the fencers decide whether the winning score will be 5 points or 15 points. This is okay. The person who achieves the winning score first is the winner. Sometimes fencers just decide to fence for practice without scoring. This is okay too.

The important thing in fencing is to try to improve. Great fencers try to improve their performance each time they fence. The best score a fencer achieves may be called their 'personal best', or PB for short. Fencing against strong opponents pushes fencers to improve their personal best. Many great fencers like Richard Kruse feel pleased when they improve their personal best result, even when an opponent wins the fight.

I may write down my score each time I fence in a special PB notebook.

The best score I achieve will be my personal best against that opponent.

I may feel pleased if I improve my personal best even if my opponent wins. Improving my personal best means I am moving closer to being the best fencer I can be. My coach will be pleased with me.

Chapter 5

Positive Self-Talk

Building Self-Confidence

Our thoughts have a critical effect on our emotions and choice of behaviour. This is the basis of all cognitive behavioural therapy. Neurotypicals experience thinking as an internal conversation, talking to ourselves, which we usually carry out silently. We describe this as self-talk. Some young people on the autism spectrum may also use self-talk but they usually talk out loud to themselves. Self-talk can be positive or negative and therefore has the ability to help or hinder our self-confidence when we face new or challenging situations.

For the young person with autism, change usually causes huge anxiety. Small changes that can be taken in a neurotypical's stride can completely terrify our young people. Even returning to a familiar day-to-day situation after a weekend, short break or holiday may result in overwhelming anxiety. Positive self-talk can be learned and practised in this situation, and in many others, as a method of self-calming, allowing the young person to refocus on the facts and knowledge they have about a situation to regain confidence and reduce their anxiety. In addition, the use of portable calming strategies that have been identified as working for the young person can reduce anxiety and improve confidence. Together these two strategies can make the young person feel more comfortable and more able to cope.

Mark experienced several episodes of feeling unsettled when he returned to his apprenticeship placement or subsequent workplace after a break. We chose the word 'unsettled' to portray what he was feeling in this situation because it was accurate, as he was neither anxious nor calm. It also allowed us to describe a return to a 'settled' state. I had a drawing conversation with him about where he worked, and having uncovered that there were no new factors within the workplace that required describing or explaining, we wrote down together several key things he knew about the workplace both from fact and past experience. I then wrote a Social Story™ describing how he could move from unsettled to settled again using his calming strategies which had worked for him before in the past. After writing the Story, I wrote factual statements, based on the information gathered for the Story, for him to recite as self-talk when faced with unsettled feelings before going in to work. I also wrote this down on a small card for him to keep in his pocket. This combination of Social Story and self-talk worked well on this and many other occasions.

Although Mark was, and is, able to use his positive self-talk statements well, it is important to note that I always explore the context of each individual situation he is experiencing anxiety with him too. This is because a familiar context may change and he may become uneasy about it, but be less able to recognise what the new context is, and importantly whether it is safe and friendly or not. Mark, like many other young people on the autism spectrum, may also become aware of a negative atmosphere but may not have the context sensitivity to truly understand the meaning behind it. So before encouraging him to use his positive self-talk statements, I gather information from the situation, and from Mark, around any changes that may have taken place. I do not want him to be using this strategy to endure an unsafe or unfriendly situation.

The first Story in this chapter is an early Story called 'What does calm down mean?' This Story has been included in my previous collection of Stories for young children (Timmins, 2016) and in my collection of Stories for school and college students (Timmins, 2017). This is not needless repetition. Reminders of calming strategies throughout life, and adaptation of them to grow with the young person with autism, are required through the lifespan due to the very high levels of anxiety experienced in our neurotypical world.

The Story describes the use of self-calming strategies. These strategies were originally chosen and used by Mark spontaneously himself and have been adapted into a portable format so that they may be accessible to use when 'unexpected things happen' away from home. I have deliberately avoided describing using strategies when 'anxious', as he may, or may not, be able to work out when he is feeling anxious. He will however certainly notice when something unexpected happens!

The second Story that follows here, a much later Story, written for a higher level of understanding, describes moving from 'unsettled to settled' in the workplace. The Story does refer to calming strategies and self-talk statements, so it is important that the young person has already understood and used both of these before reading this Story. The positive self-talk statements are written separately after this Story, and are not actually part of the Story. Positive self-talk statements frequently focus on the words, 'I can...' In contrast, Social Stories use the word 'can' with caution, only choosing it when the skill being referred to is currently within the young person's repertoire. In this example I was confident that all the self-talk statements were within Mark's capability at the time. This is an important consideration when writing self-talk statements for young people on the autism spectrum.

Linking positive self-talk statements to positive visual images can be really helpful. Many young people are strong visual thinkers. Temple Grandin, who has high-functioning autism and is a professor in animal behaviour, says, 'I think in pictures. Words are like a second language to me... When somebody speaks to me his words are instantly translated into pictures' (Grandin, 1996, p.1). I have noticed this to be the case in many children with autism. I have found that if I can link an abstract concept with a meaningful concrete visual image for the young person I may be able to engage them in a meaningful way that can be instantly recalled for future use. What seems to be important for my son and others is that the images chosen relate to an interest of theirs. For example, in Mark's case, I frequently used meerkats or penguins, which were, and continue to be, a real interest for him. Meerkats, through their behaviours, are the living embodiment of what it feels like to be highly vigilant and anxious, always on the look-out for change. They also visually demonstrate the comfort of being with family and safe friends where they rapidly relax and drop off to sleep comfortably. Watching the series *Meerkat Manor* on DVD with Mark has given me many opportunities to use characters and situations to explain feelings, emotions and the reactions of others.

The third Story included here uses images of meerkats to improve the understanding of feeling 'unsettled' when a change is happening. Of course, some children and young adults will not be able to understand analogy or the use of animal characters to illustrate a point, so each Story must be written at the cognitive level of the individual using constructs that they absolutely already understand.

What does calm down mean?

Sometimes children feel calm. Sometimes
children feel worried. Many children and
adults feel worried some of the time and
calm some of the time. This is okay.

Usually when someone is worried they try
to make themselves feel calmer. This is
called 'calming down'. People try to 'calm
down' because feeling calm is a good
comfy feeling.

People usually have a favourite way of
calming down.

My LSA takes three big breaths when she needs to calm down. This helps her think clearly when unexpected things happen

I am learning how to calm down. Learning how to calm down may help me think clearly when unexpected things happen. Four things that may help me calm down are:

1. Counting to ten penguins

2. Thinking about an episode of
   Danger Mouse

3. Feeling my hanky in my pocket

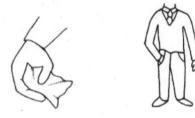

4. Asking for chill-out time.

I will work on calming down when unexpected things happen. My teacher and my LSA will be pleased with me.

Moving from unsettled to settled

Sometimes I feel settled at work. Sometimes I feel unsettled at work. Many people feel settled some of the time and unsettled some of the time.

Sometimes when I feel unsettled using my calming strategies helps me feel settled again. Sometimes using my self-talk statements quietly to myself helps too.

Thinking about what I know about the workplace also helps. My workplace is usually a safe place. The people in my workplace are usually friendly and safe people who like me. I usually know what to do in my job and my boss is usually pleased with my work. When unsure about something at work there are two people I can usually ask for help: [name] or [name].

I have felt unsettled in my workplace before and become settled again after a short time. I felt unsettled when I came back to work from a long weekend away and from holiday. I used my calming strategies and my self-talk statements to move from feeling unsettled back to feeling settled. I am learning to move from unsettled to settled.

My self-talk statements

I know this place and it is a safe place.

I know the people who work here. They are friendly and safe people who like me.

I know what to do in my job.

I know what to say in my job.

I know who I can ask for help here.

I have done this before and I can try to do it again.

Meerkats have unsettled times too

Sometimes meerkats feel settled. Usually meerkats feel settled when everything is happening just as normal and life is going peacefully according to plan.

Sometimes meerkats feel unsettled. Meerkats usually feel unsettled when changes happen within their burrow. Sometimes there is a change of schedule. The leader may decide to lead a foraging trip for food at an unexpected time of day. This usually makes the meerkats feel a little unsettled.

They still go foraging for the same length of time. They still go foraging to the same place. They still go with the same group of meerkats.

When the meerkats have foraged at the new time for several days they usually begin to feel settled again. Life soon returns to normal.

In my apprenticeship things are feeling a little unsettled. The hours I am working have moved from the morning to the afternoon. I am still going to be with the same group of people. I am still going to be working in the same place. I am still going to be doing the work I normally do.

Many people and meerkats feel unsettled when there are changes to the routine. When I have worked at the new time for several days I usually begin to feel settled again. Life soon returns to normal.

Life often has times when a person feels unsettled and times when they feel settled again. This is how life happens for all people and all meerkats.

When I feel unsettled I will try to use my self-talk and calming strategies until things feel more settled again. Life will soon return to normal.

References

Attwood, T. (2008) *The Complete Guide to Asperger's Syndrome*. London: Jessica Kingsley Publishers.

Baron-Cohen, S. (1995) *Mindblindness: An Essay on Autism and Theory of Mind*. Cambridge, MA: MIT Press.

Bowler, D.M., Gardiner, J.M. and Grice, S.J. (2000) 'Episodic memory and remembering in adults with Asperger syndrome.' *Journal of Autism and Developmental Disorders 30*, 4, 295–304.

Cornum, R. (1992) *She Went to War: The Rhonda Cornum Story*. Novato, CA: Presidio Press.

Frederickson, B. (2010) *Positivity: Groundbreaking Research to Release Your Inner Optimist and Thrive*. London: One World Publications.

Frith, U. (2003) *Autism: Explaining the Enigma* (2nd edition). Oxford: Blackwell.

Goddard, L., Dritschel, B., Robinson, S. and Howlin, P. (2014) 'Development of autobiographical memory in children with autism spectrum disorders: deficits, gains, and predictors of performance.' *Development and Psychopathology 26*, 1, 215–228.

Goldberg, M., Mostofsky, S.,Cutting, L., Mahone, E., Astor, B., Denckla, M. and Landa, R. (2005) 'Subtle Executive Impairment in Children with Autism and Children with ADHD.' *Journal of Autism and Developmental Disorders, 35*, 279.

Grandin, T. (1996) *Thinking in Pictures and Other Reports from My Life with Autism*. New York: Vintage Books.

Gray, C. (1994) *Comic Strip Conversations*. Arlington: Future Horizons.

Gray, C. (2015) *The New Social Story TM Book* (15th anniversary edition). Arlington: Future Horizons.

Harms, P., Herian, M., Krasikova, D., Vanhove, A. and Lester, P. (2013) *The Comprehensive Soldier and Family Fitness Program Evaluation. Report #4: Evaluation of Resilience Training and Mental and Behavioral Health Outcomes*. Available at http://digitalcommons.unl.edu/cgi/viewcontent.cgi?article=1009&context=pdharms (accessed on 6 April 2017).

Pennington, B.F. and Ozonoff, S. (1996). 'Executive functions and developmental psychopathology.' *Journal of Child Psychology and Psychiatry 37*, 1, 51–87.

Siebert, A. (2005) *The Resiliency Advantage*. San Francisco: Berrett-Koehler.

Simonoff, E., Pickels, A., Charman, Tony., Chandler, S., Loucas, T. and Baird, G. (2008). 'Psychiatric disorders in children with ASD: prevalence, comorbidity and associated factors in a population-derived sample.' *Journal of the American Academy of Child and Adolescent Psychiatry 47*, 8, 921–9.

Timmins, S. (2016) *Successful Social Stories™ for Young Children*. London: Jessica Kingsley Publishers.

Timmins, S. (2017) *Successful Social Stories™ for School and College Students with Autism*. London: Jessica Kingsley Publishers.

Vermeulen, P. (2012) *Autism as Context Blindness*. Kansas: AAPC.